Original title:
Inside the Walls of Wonder

Copyright © 2025 Creative Arts Management OÜ
All rights reserved.

Author: Zachary Prescott
ISBN HARDBACK: 978-1-80587-051-7
ISBN PAPERBACK: 978-1-80587-521-5

Portals of Unexpected Journeys

In a cupboard where socks like to hide,
A portal opens, my cat's taken a ride.
He stares at the wall, with one paw in the air,
I laugh as he whispers, 'Is this a fair share?'

Through a mirror, I step, looking fresh as a pear,
But my hair's turned to jelly, it's stuck everywhere!
My reflection is cackling, with glee it confides,
'Life's much more fun when you laugh at the ride.'

A door in the back seems to beckon my name,
It leads to a circus, oh this isn't a game!
I juggle with pickles while riding a goat,
And the clown shouts, 'Hey, you've still got my coat!'

A closet reveals a musical sock,
It sings out loud while it does the conga bop.
I join in the dance with a tap and a twirl,
Where else can you find such a magical whirl?

Whispers of Forgotten Dreams

In a jar, a dream sat tight,
Chasing its tail through the night.
A tickle from a passing breeze,
Chuckled soft, begging for keys.

A hat made of marshmallow fluff,
Danced with shoes that were too tough.
The moon burst out laughing aloud,
As stars spun in a silly crowd.

The Tapestry of Hidden Realms

Threads of giggles intertwine,
Spinning stories, oh so fine.
A sneaky cat that wore a tie,
Debated with a pie in the sky.

Laughter stitched in every seam,
As dragons fogged their morning dream.
They fluttered by with winks and grins,
In lands where mischief always wins.

Shadows of Curiosity

A shadow mouse with a bowtie,
Proclaimed, 'Why don't clouds ever fly?'
A silly riddle, a playful pose,
Tickled the grass and made it doze.

Bouncing questions, the air did twirl,
While fireflies danced and gave a whirl.
They laughed at questions all the same,
In a game where truth had lost its name.

The Garden of Silken Hues

In a patch of rainbow grass,
Daisies wore shades with a sass.
Lollipops bloomed beneath the moon,
Singing a silly, sugary tune.

Giggling flowers, a whimsical sight,
Bowling with bees that flew in flight.
They traded whispers, shared their sweets,
In a carnival where joy repeats.

Riddles in Dusty Corners

In a nook there's a shoe, old as time,
A sock we lost in a jar of lime.
A hat with a feather, with stories to lend,
It whispers out secrets, the walls just pretend.

Beneath the old rug, a dance floor awaits,
Where dust bunnies twirl with mismatched plates.
An uncle's old joke in a book on the shelf,
Makes me giggle and snort, oh can't help myself.

The Allure of the Unseen

There's a ghost in the attic who sings off-key,
He tries to scare pets but they just flee.
A cat with a suitcase, it dreams of a trip,
While mice plot their heist with a snack in each grip.

In shadows, the shadows play hide and seek,
With whispers of laughter that tickle the cheek.
A spoon starts to dance with a fork to its beat,
Now that is some fun, oh what a sweet treat!

Journeys through the Twilight Dreamscape

On clouds that giggle and pillows that pout,
I ride on my dreams, there's never a doubt.
A dragon with hiccups breathes bubbles of air,
While fairies argue 'bout who gets the chair.

In lands made of jelly and rivers of goo,
I conquer the marshmallows, they're leading the crew.
A snail on a skateboard, oh what a fast ride,
With friends like these, there's no need to hide.

Celestial Tides of Wonderment

Stars are just candies strewn through the night,
With wishes and giggles taking flight.
The moon likes to play peek-a-boo, see,
And occasionally trips on its own silver D.

Comets wear capes as they zoom past the sun,
Shouting hello to the planets for fun.
A nebula's canvas, it paints with a flare,
Cosmic laughter is floating up there in the air.

The Universe Within

In the box of my heart, a cat wears a hat,
Chasing tiny stars while I sit and chat.
Jellybeans dance on a marshmallow stage,
Singing silly songs, oh how they engage!

Balloons float by with secrets untold,
While gummy bears argue about being bold.
I spilled my thoughts on a cosmic kite,
Now they soar high, oh what a sight!

The Altar of Past Lives

At the shrine of my socks, a shriveled shoe,
Speaks of wild parties with a llama or two.
Cereal boxes whisper of breakfasts so grand,
Where marshmallow rainbows always take a stand.

A fish on a skateboard gives a wink and a grin,
As I ponder the lives that I've lived in a spin.
Yesterday's lunch still claims its fame,
As past adventures sit in a game!

The Whispering Labyrinth

In a maze of giggles, a gnome wears a tie,
Telling knock-knock jokes to a curious fly.
He insists that the cheese is the key to the door,
While pickles make plans for a dance on the floor.

Each corner I turn, there's a dance-off in place,
As broccoli judges with a smile on its face.
The walls seem to chuckle, the floors start to sway,
In this wacky retreat where silliness plays!

Ethereal Pages of the Heart

In a book of lost dreams, the pages flip fast,
With illustrations of monsters that shadows cast.
A cereal box hero jumps off with a cry,
Sailing through rainbows, oh me, oh my!

The heart spills its secrets with glitter and glee,
While chocolate chip cookies brew laughter for tea.
Every word is a giggle, every line is a cheer,
In this magical realm where joy's always near!

Hidden Paths of the Mind

In corners where giggles bloom,
Your thoughts may dance while making room.
A hat made of cheese, what a delight,
Furry mice join in, all dressed up tight.

Chasing dreams with a rubber band,
Silly ideas splash like the sand.
Whispers of laughter, echoes so bright,
Tickling the thoughts like a feathered kite.

The Bridge of Unfathomed Thoughts

A path of marshmallows stretches wide,
Where penguins in bow ties happily glide.
We bounce on clouds of jittery glee,
Juggling fluffy kittens, oh can't you see?

A straw hat wearing a cactus sings,
While pink elephants dance with strings.
Hopscotch on rainbows, life's a ride,
As unicorns twirl, let worries slide.

Ethereal Eclipses

When fruits wear hats, the moon takes a bow,
Bananas sigh softly, "Why not now?"
Jellybean stars twinkle so bright,
A giggle from Mars, oh what a sight!

Pajamas on clouds, dreams take their roll,
Whimsical whispers escape from a shoal.
A comical plunge in a giggle pool,
Where rules are just laughter — a universal tool.

The Echoes from the Soul's Pocket

Secret whispers from a pocketed grin,
Where giggles and socks unite with a spin.
A sprite with a trumpet sings soft and low,
While shadows in hats plan a comedy show.

In the realm of socks, dreams take flight,
Slippers and slippers, oh what a sight.
Chasing giggles through cushions galore,
This whimsical world never leaves you bored.

The Opal Dreamcatcher

A spider spun a web so rare,
It caught the dreams that floated there.
But then a breeze gave them a spin,
Now cats chase dreams, and dogs wear grins.

The opal glowed with hues so bright,
It tickled thoughts and sparked delight.
When nightfall hit, the dreams took flight,
And danced with owls till morning light.

In corners dark, the fairies play,
Telling jokes at break of day.
With giggles soft, they float around,
In this odd world where fun is found.

So if you see a dream take wing,
Just laugh along, and hear it sing.
For every night's a silly show,
Where giggles guide the dreams we throw.

Time's Secret Chamber

In a drawer where tick-tocks rest,
Lies a clock that's truly blessed.
It wears a hat and tells bad jokes,
While teasing all the wandering folks.

The past and future come to play,
In card games that last all day.
With silly bets on what's to come,
Time tricks us all; it's quite the pun!

Then suddenly, a rabbit hops,
With pockets full of lollipops.
He shares a laugh with passing time,
While munching candy, all is fine.

If you peek in that secret space,
You'll find the silliest of grace.
For every tick is filled with cheer,
And seconds laugh, so lend an ear!

Threads of the Cosmic Loom

In a workshop up among the stars,
They weave the light with silly spars.
With every thread a tale is spun,
Of dancing comets having fun.

A loom that hums with cosmic pride,
Threads tickle space in a playful ride.
As galaxies swirl in a giggling race,
The fabric of time holds a smirking face.

Spiders weave with giggly grace,
While meteors join the grand embrace.
They each throw in their bestest cheer,
Binding the cosmos year by year.

So if you gaze at stars above,
And feel that tingle, that spark of love.
Remember, it's all one grand jest,
In the tapestry where laughter rests.

The Architecture of Imagination

In a city built of dreams and schemes,
The towers sway like dancing beams.
Each wall can giggle, each door can sing,
As dreams create the wildest fling.

A bridge of thoughts connects the land,
Where silly shadows take a stand.
With every step, a jest unfolds,
In this wise land where laughter molds.

The clouds wear hats, the sun a tie,
Banters amongst a bright blue sky.
With every corner, surprise awaits,
And joy unlocks the fanciest gates.

So wander through this joyous place,
Where fun is found in every space.
In the architecture of delight,
Imagination dances through the night.

Dreams Beyond the Echo

Bouncing thoughts like rubber balls,
Chasing shadows down the halls.
Giggles dance upon the breeze,
Tickle fights with pillows, please!

Whispers hide in creaky floors,
Wobbly chairs and secret doors.
Jellybeans that sing and hum,
Where's my snack? Oh, here it comes!

Silly hats that make us tall,
Puppy barks that giggle and sprawl.
Every turn a new surprise,
Silly grins and starry skies.

Frogs that wear a suit and tie,
Painting rainbows in the sky.
Joyful chaos fills the scene,
In this land where we can dream.

The Hidden Nexus

Sneaky gnomes with tiny feet,
Steal your lunch, oh what a feat!
A lizard sings a funky tune,
Underneath a laughing moon.

Bouncing buttons, twirling toys,
Clocks that tick with silly noise.
Mice in capes prepare to fly,
Watch them leap! Oh my, oh my!

A jumpy pen that writes a joke,
Giggling clouds make laughter poke.
Jumbling dreams, they spin and spin,
In this world, we just dive in!

Dancing socks upon the floor,
Peek-a-boo from every door.
Curly fries that tell a tale,
Here's a smile, without fail!

The Cradle of Lost Realities

Yonder lies the magic dust,
In a jar marked 'playful rust.'
Marshmallow clouds and jelly beans,
Fluffy dreams in rainbow scenes.

Twirling teacups, spinning cheer,
Silly signs that shout, 'Hello, dear!'
A kazoo plays a funky beat,
Would you like a dancing seat?

Wandering through this wiggly maze,
Laughter echoes in a daze.
A tuba twirls—a funny sight,
Bubblegum pops add to the light.

Wobbly elephants paint the air,
With sprinkles of joy everywhere.
In this cradle of the wild,
Every heart is still a child.

The Palette of a Dreamer's Heart

Colors splash upon the wall,
Plenty of giggles, such a ball!
Crayons dreaming, making art,
Every scribble, a joyful start.

Pastels hum a silly tune,
Painting sunflowers, pink balloons.
Chalk-dust fairies twirl and play,
As laughter lights the cloudy day.

A canvas sings, oh what a sight,
Swirling shapes in pure delight.
Splashes echo through the air,
Creativity is everywhere!

Dancing brushes, winking paints,
Silly stories of colorful saints.
In the heart where laughter starts,
Dreams burst forth in clever parts.

Curiosities Behind Closed Doors

There's a cat wearing glasses, it reads a book,
In the corner, a spoon starts to cook.
A chair laughs loud, it rocks with glee,
While a shy old lamp winks secretly.

A mirror that snickers, reflects a grin,
As clouds in the cupboard roll out and spin.
The rug tells jokes in a ticklish tone,
And the clock sneezes, 'Time's not alone!'

Each painting whispers, secrets to share,
While a mischievous gnome plays tricks in the air.
The walls ebb and flow with giggles and guffaws,
A whimsical kingdom with its own little laws.

Here, each odd treasure invites you to play,
Such wonderful wonders await every day.
A world of delight, so cheekily strange,
In this funny abode, we merrily range.

The Tapestry of Forgotten Dreams

In a quilt sewn with laughter, a fox does a dance,
A fish wears a top hat, it's taking a chance.
With each thread unraveling a tale of delight,
Where rainbows are sandwiches, oh what a sight!

Under the stars, a shoe starts to sing,
A donut plays drums, and the curtains take wing.
The dreams that were lost take a trip to the moon,
While slippers do ballet to a whimsical tune.

In this patchwork of wishes, a cactus wears shoes,
And kittens in pajamas have nothing to lose.
The tapestry shimmers with colors so wild,
As it giggles and whispers, just like a child.

Forgotten and cherished, they twirl and they spin,
Each memory dances, bringing joy from within.
So in this odd world, let your dreams take flight,
With fabric of fun, we'll soar into the night.

Mysterious Pathways of the Mind

Wander through corridors where laughter roams free,
A hat on a turtle suggests, 'Follow me!'
With doors made of candy, and walls full of songs,
This zany adventure, where nothing feels wrong.

A dandelion whispers secrets as you go,
While socks hold a summit, discussing the flow.
Fish on bicycles ride past a wise tree,
And clouds play hopscotch, oh what glee to see!

Inside this brain maze, squirrels hold a race,
With giggles and wiggles, they zip every space.
A chimera spins tales to warm up the night,
As laughter erupts and thoughts take to flight.

So skip down these pathways, let your spirit unwind,
For joy blooms in places where thoughts intertwine.
This merry adventure, take part if you dare,
With silly distractions that dance in the air.

Ephemeral Journeys Beyond the Veil

A ghost on a skateboard zooms past the moon,
While marshmallow clouds hum a cheery tune.
With a wink and a nod, they tumble and swirl,
In this vibrant realm where odd dreams unfurl.

In the distance, a dragon knits with a tree,
While fairies on bicycles giggle with glee.
Each shadow tells stories in whimsical ways,
With laughter that lingers and joy that stays.

A merry-go-round spins with a bounce in its step,
As flamingos in slippers do their dance prep.
The wind shares a secret that tickles the ear,
A chuckle erupts, casting away every fear.

So join this adventure, where whimsy prevails,
In whimsical currents, let joy set your sails.
For ephemeral journeys spark laughter and cheer,
In a carnival of wonders, the magic is here.

The Sanctuary of Lost Thoughts

In a place where socks disappear,
I ponder why my keys aren't here.
Thoughts bounce like a rubber ball,
At times, they're big, then they're quite small.

Chasing dreams that fly away,
They giggle and they love to play.
A lollipop of yesterday's fun,
Melted now, oh where has it run?

Jokes linger in the curtain's shade,
While my to-do list starts to fade.
A treasure map of silly things,
Where laughter dances, and joy sings.

Whispers hide in the creaky stairs,
Suggesting mischief in the air.
I catch a glimpse of a fluffy cat,
As it plots with a hat and a spat!

Harmonies in the Depths of Silence

In quiet rooms, a sneeze will play,
A symphony of night and day.
Crickets chirp their awkward tune,
As I dance like a clumsy cartoon.

Dust motes waltz through sunlit beams,
Laughing at my wildest dreams.
A sock puppet with eyes so bright,
Looks serious, but what a sight!

Echoes tease with ticklish rhymes,
Turning chores into fun times.
With every silence, a joke grows,
Like silly mice in party clothes.

Whispers tangle with playful glee,
As secrets spill from a woodsy tree.
The quiet cracks with giggling spright,
Who knew silence could feel so light?

Treasures Buried Beneath Perception

The map says X, but I can't find,
The hidden loot that haunts my mind.
With shovels made from plastic spoons,
We dig through dreams, not ancient runes.

Beneath the dust, a button gleams,
A relic from my childhood dreams.
A rubber duck, a trinket rare,
Who knew I was a treasure bear?

In every mess, a gem appears,
Sparkling bright through laughter and tears.
A wobbly kite, a moldy snack,
What secrets lie within that pack?

So join the hunt, come take a look,
At every squishy, silly nook.
The greatest finds are full of cheer,
Come dig with me, there's nothing to fear!

A Mosaic of Fading Memories

Fragments glimmer like broken glass,
Remnants of a silly class.
A cupcake fight, a paper plane,
Laughing 'til we danced in rain.

Old photographs with goofy grins,
Reciting tales where laughter spins.
Red balloons that floated high,
Shriek with joy, and then say bye!

Tickling past all the things we lost,
In every giggle, we count the cost.
A castle made from couch cushions,
Turns to laughter, our best musings.

Memories swirl like autumn leaves,
In the wind where mischief weaves.
So grab a piece, come share the fun,
In this mosaic, we are one!

The Paradox of Unfolding Light

In shadows deep where giggles grow,
A light bulb flickers, on it goes.
The jokes spill forth like milk mispoured,
While wisdom sleeps, and puns are scored.

A cat in boots with dreams of flight,
Chased wispy tales in the day's twilight.
Laughter trapped in echoes' weave,
Tickles the air; who'd dare believe?

Bright colors clash like clumsy fools,
Their dances praised in jest-filled schools.
A paradox wrapped in a riddle's grip,
With each step forward, we slip and trip.

So raise your glass to the curious side,
Where laughter's a secret that can't hide.
For in this place, with a giggle or two,
The light's unfolding brings joy anew.

Epiphanies Amidst the Quiet

In quiet nooks where whispers play,
A teapot chuckles, holding sway.
The cookies scheme with chocolate chips,
In a hasty way, they plot their trips.

The sofa grins with a twitchy seam,
While socks collaborate in a crazy dream.
Synchronized in our still refrain,
A dance of thoughts like a loose champagne.

The moments linger, awkward yet sweet,
As moths flirt shyly with the heat.
It's an epiphany wrapped in a sigh,
Where secrets bloom and silly sparks fly.

So take a pause in this quiet spree,
Embrace the laugh of absurdity.
For in these musings, layered and spry,
Laughter unfolds; it's no lie.

The Rift Between Worlds

A toaster dreamed of cosmic toast,
While cats discussed the value of ghosts.
In rifts between, the spoons aligned,
They charted paths in a paper bind.

The floorboards creak with comedic flair,
As socks go missing without a care.
Two worlds collide in a giggling spin,
A dance-off started; let the games begin.

Muffins sprout with faces so sly,
Winking at muffins who wonder why.
In the rift, all logic goes to sleep,
As pancakes conspire and secrets creep.

Raise a toast to the blend, the delight,
Where laughter flows and shines so bright.
For in this rift, with a chuckle or two,
The worlds collide in a whimsical view.

The Starlit Occult

Beneath the stars where shadows dance,
A squirrel conspired, given a chance.
It whispered secrets to the moon,
As owls giggled with their own tune.

Candles flicker with a playful jest,
Churned butter dreams put to the test.
In the starlit cloak, bizarre sights unfold,
With laughter spun from the stories told.

The hats are levitating, oh what a sight!
With rubber ducks taking their flight.
The occult isn't dark; it's filled with cheer,
Where the bizarre is welcomed near.

So join the party, let's not be shy,
With ghosts and fairies, we'll all apply.
In this starlit whirl, the fun won't halt,
For the night's a charade in the starlit occult.

Intricate Labyrinths of Imagination

In a maze of thought so wild,
I stumbled on a cat who smiled.
He wore a hat, was sipping tea,
And said, "Why not just dance with me?"

A jester jumped, a rabbit pranced,
With every twist, they laughed and chanced.
They ordered snacks from clouds above,
And declared pie is a sign of love!

Colors zigzagged in playful flight,
As squirrels debated the stars at night.
I chose a door marked with a sign,
"Caution! Here, all rabbits dine!"

So in this world, we're free to play,
With every turn, it's a holiday.
Join the fun, don't be a bore,
For laughter lives just through that door!

Revelations from the Quiet Nook

In a corner where shadows speak,
A goldfish wore a monocle, so sleek.
He whispered tales of rainbow fries,
And taught me how to levitate pies!

A chair began to twirl and spin,
Inviting me to dance and grin.
The tables sang a jazzy tune,
While clocks kept time with quite a swoon.

An octopus served popcorn dreams,
With jellybeans as far as beams.
He said, "Let's paint the walls with sound,
And make the echoes dance around!"

In this nook, where laughter flares,
A world of whimsy always cares.
So hush, my friend, and take a seat,
The quiet nook is quite the treat!

Fantasies Roaming in Silent Echoes

In silent echoes, whispers bloom,
A kangaroo jumps across the room.
With every hop, confetti flies,
And unicorns spark joy in their eyes!

They chat with pixies, sipping dew,
While cupcakes frolic, oh so few.
A dragon in a tutu twirls,
Declaring, "Life's for all the whirls!"

The shadows giggle, lights entwine,
As everyone grabs a glass of brine.
A mermaid pops up just for kicks,
And teaches us her favorite tricks.

So let your mind drift and soar,
In realms of fun, seek and explore.
For in the echoes, laughter calls,
A bright adventure awaits us all!

Glimpses of the Uncharted Landscape

In lands where jellybeans grow on trees,
A butterfly sneezed, but it was a breeze.
It tickled flowers that laughed out loud,
And brought a rainbow, bright and proud!

A turtle raced against a snail,
With a tiny ship made from a pail.
As they sailed on streams of soda pop,
The fish cheered loudly, "Don't you stop!"

A cloud in pink socks danced on air,
Singing, "Life's fabulous, do you dare?"
It taught the stars to jump and play,
While moonbeams joined the fun in sway.

So grab your gear, let's roam this place,
Each glance revealing a funny face.
In this landscape, joy is grand,
In every corner, something unplanned!

Alchemy of the Infinite

In a lab of stars and giggles,
Elixirs bubble, like silly wiggles.
A recipe for laughter, a hint of glee,
Mix with a dash of whimsy, and let it be!

Jars of dreams line the wooden shelf,
Each one whispers, 'Do it yourself!'
Turn whims into potions, stir them right,
Pour them in mugs, let nonsensicals ignite.

Bottles with labels that simply say 'Fun',
Sip them with friends 'til the day is done.
We'll dance with the shadows, we'll sing with the light,
Spinning around in our own merry flight.

A sprinkle of joy, just a pinch of chaos,
With every chuckle, we're winking at ethos.
So come join the ruckus, let's bake some mirth,
In this alchemy, there's never a dearth!

The Mural of Daydreams

On a canvas of clouds, let's splash some color,
Draw sassy squirrels and a laughable scholar.
Unicorns prance in pajamas so neat,
While broccoli dances with two left feet.

A brush dipped in sunshine, a stroke of delight,
Paint a bear in a top hat, now wouldn't that be a sight?
A rainbow's end leads to a genie's café,
Serving up coffee brewed in a whimsical way.

With each brushstroke, giggles erupt,
Capturing moments, cheerfully corrupt.
A scene of squirrels hosting a tea party grand,
Inviting the moonlight to lend it a hand.

The mural hums with stories unknown,
Each character struts, in their joy overblown.
So grab a paintbrush, come join the spree,
In this daydream mural, we're wild and free!

Silhouettes of What Could Be

In the hallway of hopes, shadows play,
Chasing each other in a cheeky ballet.
A hippo in slippers, a frog on a stage,
Shouting out jokes, all the world's a cage.

Each silhouette whispers a tale, oh so strange,
Of comets who tango and stars that exchange.
They wobble like jelly, they jive with flair,
Dancing on ceilings, with mischief to spare.

The walls are alive with soft echoing dreams,
Where humor tickles like bright sunbeams.
A cat in a top hat, a roguish disguise,
Stealing the spotlight in a world full of lies.

When night kisses day, and shadows combine,
We'll laugh at the quirks of this intricate line.
So peek at the shadows, see what you find,
In silhouettes waiting for you to unwind!

The Portal of Hidden Glories

Through a door made of giggles, let's tumble and fall,
Into realms of the quirky, where fun is the call.
Watch pizza birds soar with strings of spaghetti,
In this land of delight, everything's ready!

A portal of humor, a corridor wide,
Where mysteries waltz and whimsy can glide.
A bouncy castle shaped like a giant shoe,
Invites the clowns over for hotdogs to chew.

Every step leads to laughs, oh can you believe?
With each twist and turn, there's joy to receive.
Jellybeans chatter, and marshmallows cheer,
Celebrating the laughter that brings us all near.

So leap through the portal, let giggles ensue,
In the realm of the silly, where dreams come true.
Here's to the hidden, the quirks we adore,
In this magical space, there's always much more!

Revelations from the Heart of the Prism

In a corner, a sock plays hide and seek,
A pancake flips, then it falls off the peak.
The cat wears a hat, struts with great pride,
While the goldfish judges from the other side.

In the fridge, a pickle has declared a dance,
A spilled drink giggles, it takes quite a chance.
The mouse brings cookies, always a delight,
As the toaster hums softly, sparks taking flight.

A broom with ambitions dreams of a race,
Chasing dust bunnies at an unbeatable pace.
A window whispers, full of secrets to tell,
While a spoon and a fork start to break out of shell.

What chaos unfolds in this quirky domain,
Where laughter is binding, and silliness reigns.
Each corner reveals a story anew,
In this prism of life, where wonders ensue.

A Symphony of Color and Sound

A paintbrush strums on the canvas so wide,
While crayons tap dance, no need to hide.
A trumpet gets jealous of pastel tunes,
As laughter erupts with the glow of the moons.

The walls sing along in a colorful glee,
Echoes of colors, vibrant and free.
A tuba's bright notes lead a feathered parade,
With rainbows and rhythm, a whimsical charade.

A drawstring of laughter pulls at the seams,
While marbles roll softly, weaving their dreams.
Electric blue notes flicker and spin,
As the symphony revels in chaos within.

The audience chuckles, they clap with delight,
For it's not every day that colors take flight.
In the heart of the scene, a mirth so profound,
Creating a chorus of whimsy and sound.

The Guardian of Unspoken Tales

In a library, whispers tangle like hair,
Books peek through glasses with a knowing glare.
The quill has a secret, it scribbles a plot,
While paper clips form a musical knot.

A lamp hums a tune, it flickers with pride,
As pencils debate on where truth might reside.
Bookmarks conspire, revealing new words,
While the pages flutter like excited birds.

A chair winks slyly, waiting for a guest,
With cushions that giggle, they're cozy and blessed.
The clock makes a fuss, moving time with a laugh,
As laughter erupts in this literary staff.

In shadows and light, tales weave and unwind,
Guardians of stories, both silly and kind.
Every corner whispers of mysteries yet told,
In this merry place where imagination unfolds.

Fragments of a Luminous Past

Once a teapot dreamed of being a star,
Now it's a relic with tales from afar.
A kettle's whistling, a symphony sweet,
As the spoons share gossip, it's quite the treat.

Old photographs giggle, reliving their days,
While dusty old shoes dance in a daze.
A clock grumbles softly, holding back years,
As the laughter of moments washes away tears.

A scarf tells adventures of chilly nights,
While the fridge hums of forgotten delights.
Fragments of laughter stuck on the wall,
In this treasure of memories, fun reigns for all.

Bottles of soda shake up their pride,
While the cupboard conspires, feeling quite wide.
Luminous echoes revive forgotten trends,
In the realm of the past, where the laughter never ends.

Enigmas Masked in Light

In a room where shadows dance,
A cat in a hat leads the prance.
With riddles crafted in glee,
Even the lamp seems to flee.

A jester jumps on a tall chair,
Waving his socks in the air.
Giggles bounce off the white walls,
As laughter echoes, it calls.

A lamp that squirts juice from its light,
A shoe that thinks it's a kite.
Balloon animals sip from a cup,
Swirling around, never give up.

So come join this curious spree,
Where silliness roams wild and free.
Every corner whispers a jest,
In this chamber of humorous zest.

Reveries of the Forgotten Path

Beneath the tree, a squirrel sings,
Dressed up like Elvis, with gold rings.
The path is paved with popsicle sticks,
As ants play chess with their wooden tricks.

There's a fountain bubbling with soda pop,
A dancing mouse doing a flip-flop.
Each stone on the trail hums a tune,
As shadows gather to croon at noon.

In a field where daisies wear hats,
Imaginative llamas chat with bats.
With every step, chuckles arise,
As butterflies plot their own surprise.

This journey leads to a land so bright,
Where even the trees have a funny slight.
Lost in laughter along this route,
Come join the whimsy, there's no doubt!

Echoes of Enchantment

A wizard's wand made of spaghetti,
Sends shadows dancing, oh so petty.
With garlic bread as his grand steed,
Chasing fairies with a cheesy deed.

A bubbling cauldron of hot chocolate,
Turns the gloom to a sweet pocket.
Chocolate frogs leap with a grin,
On croaky toads, they all begin.

Rainbow fish wear peculiar hats,
And sing duets with dancing gnats.
Each wave brings jesters, silly and bright,
This magic world is a true delight.

So let's toast with cupcakes, my friend,
To the echoes of joy that never end.
In this jolly realm, freedom's the key,
Where giggles abound and spirits run free.

Secrets Beneath the Surface

In the pond, bubbles share their tales,
While ducks wear boots and ride on snails.
The frogs hold court with a silly air,
Joking about the fish's hair.

A turtle in glasses reads a book,
Catching the sun with every nook.
With witty puns, the lilies giggle,
As the breeze makes the tall grass wiggle.

Among the reeds, secrets take flight,
As fireflies glow like stars at night.
Each splash of water brings a surprise,
As laughter twinkles in their eyes.

Dive deep and discover the mirth,
In this splashy land where dreams give birth.
Every ripple reveals something grand,
In the chuckles that dance on the sand.

The Canvas of Unwritten Stories

A cat in a hat with a very big grin,
Dances on paper where stories begin.
The ink spills out giggles, painting the air,
While squirrels debate if it's fair to declare.

A frog with a dream wears a crown made of toast,
Dreams of a castle, he brags to his host.
With crayons for swords, they duel 'neath the sun,
In a whimsical world where mischief is fun.

The clouds gossip tales draped in fluffy white hue,
As the rabbit wears sneakers, and hops straight on cue.
Each brush stroke a giggle, each splatter a jest,
In this land of the silly, they laugh like the best.

So shake off your worries, let laughter ignite,
Join the parade of the curious night.
In the canvas of dreams, where oddities reign,
We'll splash in the colors, and dance in the rain.

Phantoms of the Unseen

Ghosts play chess with a laugh and a grin,
While shadows tell secrets of mischief and sin.
With a flicker and zap, they vanish in haze,
Leaving only echoes of their playful ways.

A phantom's pet parrot squawks jokes from the night,
While the dishes all clatter, beg for a bite.
Through windows wide open, they sneak in the fun,
Creating a ruckus until day is begun.

In the corners where cobwebs weave tales of delight,
The specters of laughter join in every fright.
They tangle with brooms and then step on a rake,
As the echoes of giggles make the hallways shake.

So fear not the shadows, embrace all the sound,
For in whispers of laughter, true spirits are found.
In a realm where the funny outshines every scream,
The phantoms are friendly, living in dreams.

The Music of Enchanted Realities

A piano made of jelly plays tunes of delight,
While the spoons on the table start dancing outright.
The notes bounce around like a game of charades,
With laughter and rhythm that never just fades.

A tap with a rabbit, in a coat quite absurd,
Leads a waltz with the moon and a drowsy old bird.
With maracas made out of candy and cheer,
They sway through the night, bringing joy without fear.

The symphony swirls through a field of bright blooms,
As butterflies chuckle and dance with their tunes.
With every soft giggle, a melody spins,
In a concert of whimsy, where the laughter begins.

So let's raise our voices, sing loud with the stars,
Join the band of the curious, forgetting our scars.
In this tune of the night, where joy knows no end,
We'll waltz with the funny, our heartfelt best friend.

Realm of Promise and Illusion

A realm where the clocks only tick when you smile,
And candy canes grow in a curious style.
The trees tell you jokes as you walk by their roots,
And the rivers briskly sing tunes in neat flutes.

Here, shadows play tag while the sun takes a nap,
While clouds toss confetti from their fluffy cap.
An octopus juggles bright stars in the air,
And the daisies hold hands in a merry affair.

The puzzles crack riddles, laughing with glee,
As a tiger wears shoes made of pink guava tea.
It's a party of dreams where oddities gleam,
In a world full of whimsy, nothing's as it seems.

So dive into laughter, let it be your guide,
In a land where enchantment and silliness collide.
Together we'll explore this strange, joyous creation,
In the realm where fun lives, without hesitation.

The Alchemist's Reverie

In long lab coats, they dance and twirl,
Mixing potions with a crazy whirl.
A new brew made of socks and stew,
Turns the cat into a pink kangaroo.

With beakers bubbling, they laugh at fate,
Gold from lead? Oh, just wait!
But oops! A rat rides a dinosaur,
Now, who's the alchemist? Who's the lore?

Cackles echo through the beady night,
As chaos blooms in pure delight.
Who knew that giggles could ignite a flame,
To spark a potion with no one to blame?

The sun peeks in, a witness so sly,
To the madness brewed beneath the sky.
Bubbles burst with each hearty cheer,
In a lab where logic disappears!

Intimacy with the Abyss

Down in the depths where shadows play,
Lurks a monster who dreams in gray.
He wears a hat and sings a tune,
While juggling cheese sticks under the moon.

No one knows quite where he's been,
Befriending ghosts with a cheeky grin.
Together they plot to scare a cat,
But all he does is purr and nap.

The abyss holds secrets, odd and sweet,
Like dancing fish in shoes on their feet.
With each swish, they shimmy and sway,
Making the darkness a happy ballet.

So when you tread near the edge of night,
Don't fear the giggles, embrace the might.
For even the depths can hold a laugh,
In the company of whimsy's craft.

Threads of Celestial Whimsy

Stitching stars into a quilt of dreams,
Where unicorns nap and moonbeams beam.
Hearts and sparkles float in the air,
While comets juggle without a care.

A flying fish wears a crown of thyme,
As crickets serenade with a funky rhyme.
Together they weave a bright parade,
In a universe where jokes are made.

Buttons that giggle and thread that sings,
Create a magic that pulls on strings.
If laughter's the fabric that binds us tight,
Then let's dance on clouds and take flight!

So gather your wishes, let them unfold,
Shared in this tapestry, shiny and bold.
In a place where whimsy reigns supreme,
Every stich is a laugh, every thread a dream.

The Haiku from Another Realm

A fish in a hat,
Recites nonsense like a pro,
With a wink it splats.

Unicorns at tea,
Sipping laughter with a grin,
Peeled bananas flee.

Monkeys spin in flight,
Chasing clouds made out of cheese,
Light as a warm kite.

Ghosts tell silly tales,
Of pirates who wore bright shoes,
On board ships with sails.

The Veil of Infinite Possibilities

There once was a door that wouldn't unlock,
With a sign that read, "It's just a big rock!"
The key turned and twisted, then fell from my hand,
I shouted, "Who needs plans? Let's start a band!"

In the garden of dreams, I planted my shoe,
With hopes it would grow into something brand new.
But it sprouted a hat that flew off like a kite,
Now that is a fashion blunder, isn't it right?

The tables would dance when I walked in the room,
And the chairs would all giggle, bursting with gloom.
But I told them, "Dear friends, let's dance 'til we fall,
For laughter and joy make the best kind of hall!"

So heed not the logic that keeps you confined,
Embrace the absurdities, they're one of a kind.
For life's like a circus, just hop on the ride,
Climb high with the monkeys, your fears set aside!

The Conductor of Starry Tales

There's a man in a suit, leading flutes from the moon,
With a baton made of stardust, he hums to a tune.
He tickles the skies with a wink and a jest,
Puppies dream about him, thinking he's the best.

He marches on comets with a skip and a hop,
While planets do pirouettes, never a stop.
His orchestra lively, they play on a whim,
The sun does a solo, while the stars laugh and grin.

With a bow, he commands each bright heavenly note,
A serenade drifts from a heavenly boat.
And the meteors chorus, "What a marvelous play!"
We giggle and cheer as they dance our way.

So come, take a seat, join this cosmic charade,
Where giggles and harmonies are whimsically laid.
Life's stage is a marvel with laughter and glee,
Let's conduct our own stories, you and me!

The Chakra of Unseen Horizons

In a garden of wishes where time likes to play,
A dandelion sneezed, and it blew me away.
I floated on wishes, I danced on the breeze,
As squirrels offered snacks while I begged for some cheese.

There's a cat with a top hat, he counts every star,
He insists that each one is his pet from afar.
With whiskers a-jingle, he shares all his dreams,
While the fireflies chuckle, bursting at the seams.

I find my zen space in a pile of bright socks,
With the yoga I'm doing, I'm bending like clocks.
Galaxies giggle, as I wobble and sway,
But I say with a grin, "It's just my own way!"

Wandering through colors that twirl and they spin,
With laughter as currency, I toss it like kin.
The horizon invites me, with wonders unseen,
Join me in this show, it's a whimsical scene!

The Elysian Chamber

In a chamber of giggles where broccoli sings,
The spoons play the violin, oh, what funny things!
The curtains made of candy, they flutter and sway,
While the chairs tell you secrets in a silly relay.

A parrot named Chuckles wears spectacles bright,
He puts on a show every Tuesday night.
He dances on tables, confetti in tow,
While cake serves the punchline, and everyone's glow.

"Come sit, enjoy stories," says the jester of fate,
With jokes made of marshmallows, they're really first-rate.
We'll tickle the ivories of laughter and song,
In this wondrous chamber, where nothing feels wrong.

So bring in your laughter, let the joy fill the air,
For the Elysian space is delightful and rare.
Let's laugh until dawn as the moon takes a bow,
In this kooky old chamber, let's celebrate now!

Tales Stitched in Time's Fabric

In a town where clocks dance with glee,
A cat tells tales of a cup of tea.
The baker's dough rises to the sky,
While squirrels plot schemes on the sly.

A shoe that squeaks tells secrets anew,
As children chase shadows, both old and true.
The sun winks at cows grazing near,
With cupcakes that giggle, oh dear, oh dear!

When the wind pulls pranks on the old oak tree,
Laughter escapes as bees buzz with spree.
Fairies brush dust off their worn-out wings,
And dreams come alive with the joy that it brings.

So sip on that tea while the clocks tick away,
Let's dance with the cat, come, what do you say?
In this stitched-together whimsy so bright,
We'll twirl through the tales 'til the stars say goodnight.

The Allure of Unseen Corridors

In hallways where shadows wear tall hats,
A squirrel recites poetry to sleeping cats.
The laughter of paintings echoes through air,
As a broom does the cha-cha with precise flair.

A door creaks open to reveal a maze,
While trombones serenade in sunbeam rays.
The chairs engage in a gossip-filled chat,
And the lamps flicker softly, 'It's getting late, rat!'

In hidden nooks where the dust bunnies dwell,
A spaghetti monster sings like a bell.
Pineapples lounge, sipping tea by the fire,
While the curtain pulls tales of a young sock's desire.

As echoes of giggles roam wild and free,
Join us for tea, it's as fun as can be.
When corridors twist with a wink and a grin,
Adventure awaits—let the laughter begin!

Marvels When the Stars Align

Under a moon that's a bit too bright,
Aliens play tag with meteors at night.
The stars twinkle secrets like old best friends,
While talking pancakes tell tales with no ends.

A comet swings by for a dance on a whim,
And the owl hoots lyrics that sound like a hymn.
The planets all gather for a game of charades,
While cosmos spill laughter like worn-out parades.

Jelly beans float in a sugary stream,
As unicorns prance through each glittering beam.
The sun shakes its rays in a fit of delight,
And dogs on the moon bark at dreams taking flight.

So let's toast the night with wiggles and cheer,
For when stars align, it's a scene so clear!
In a cosmic carnival no one can miss,
Join the merriment, this is pure bliss!

Veiled Mysteries of the Heart

In the garden where giggles sprout like vines,
A snail writes poems about love's designs.
The roses wear hats made of twinkling dew,
While whispers of wind weave the old and the new.

A puzzling frog croaks with wisdom so loud,
As a moonbeam dresses the night in a shroud.
The daffodils dance in five-four time,
And melodies bloom like bells in their prime.

Chocolates with secrets begin to confide,
While heartbeats play hopscotch, no need to hide.
The cheese is quite funky and has a soft heart,
As pudding debates what is art from the start.

So laugh with the flowers, let joy take its part,
In this whimsical waltz of the veiled, beating heart.
Embrace the quirks woven tender and sweet,
In mysteries found where the silly's complete.

Lanterns of the Soul's Journey

With lanterns bright and tunes so spry,
We dance in circles, oh my, oh my!
An octopus leads with tentacle flair,
As giggles float in the midnight air.

A bearded dragon wears a cap,
He claims he's slept through every nap.
While gummy bears roll down the street,
In a sticky race, they can't be beat.

Funky hats upon our heads,
With mismatched shoes, we dance in threads.
The moon winks at our quirky show,
"Who wears pajamas? We do, you know!"

With each soft glow, our laughter grows,
In tangled tales, imagination flows.
So grab a lantern, let's skip along,
Where silliness dances and dreams belong.

The Celestial Library

In shelves of stars, the books all sigh,
A wizard sneezes, and glitter flies high.
The tales of cats who long to sing,
In a universe where tigers wear bling.

A librarian elf juggles fluffy pies,
While owls hoot calculus from the skies.
With each dusty tome, a giggle escapes,
As hedgehogs spin tales in colorful capes.

Monkeys throw popcorn in the reading nook,
While giraffes strain to read a cookbook.
"Don't eat the pages, they squeak!" we plead,
In this library filled with whimsical need.

A bookworm winks with surprise in his eyes,
While cosmic fish play musical chimes.
So come join the fun, it's never a bore,
In this library realm, there's always more!

Paths of Radiant Visions

On paths of light, we jump and prance,
With unicorns leading our merry dance.
A rainbow slips on a slippery slide,
While cupcakes giggle, they just can't hide.

With marshmallow pops as walking sticks,
We stumble over stones that make us tick.
A wise old frog croaks jokes with glee,
As dragonflies buzz like cups of tea.

In fields of mushrooms the size of cars,
We gather moonbeams, we spin and are stars.
With every hop, quirks and quirks anew,
As kites made of laughter drift past the blue.

So follow the trails of silly delight,
Where giggles and grins shine ever so bright.
In the land of mirth, where dreams take flight,
We dance 'til the dawn, in glowing starlight.

The Echo Chamber of Thought

In a chamber of echoes, we lose our minds,
With thoughts that bounce like silly winds.
A chicken arrives on roller skates,
Clucking philosophical debates!

Boisterous ideas fly from each wall,
Like bouncing balls that never fall.
What do pillows really dream about?
A stuffed bear whispers, "Let's sort it out!"

In this realm where wacky thoughts break free,
We discuss why toasters can't climb a tree.
Each echo returns with a giggling twist,
"Do socks dream of shoes?" the echoes insist.

So join the chaos, let laughter unfold,
In this chamber where nonsense is gold.
Each thought we share makes the world feel bright,
In a cacophony of charm and delight.

Echoes of Enchantment

In a room full of hats, they danced with delight,
A rabbit in slippers, a curious sight.
With waltzing bananas and singing bread,
Who knew that the toaster could tickle your head?

Laughter erupted as spoons took a bow,
The jellybeans laughed, 'What's going on now?'
A cat in a cape flew right through the air,
Chasing a pencil with fabulous flair.

Time slipped away while the clock wore a grin,
Eggs tap-danced lightly, it must be a win.
In the midst of the giggles, a puppy did twirl,
With cupcakes and carrots, the sweetest of pearls.

When day turned to dusk, they all took a seat,
To trade silly stories and snacks that were sweet.
Each echo of laughter bounced high off the walls,
In this realm of delight, joy forever enthralls.

Secrets in the Silken Shadows

In a corner that whispered, a curtain swayed,
While shadows made shapes, not a bit afraid.
With a wink, a chair jumped right off the floor,
Said, 'Join in the fun! There are laughs to explore!'

A sneaky old turtle played hide and seek,
While curtains could giggle, and tables could speak.
With whispers of mischief in every dark nook,
The teapot was plotting, writing a book.

A jester flipped pancakes, one flew to the moon,
In this realm of giggles, the humor's a boon.
The dust bunnies danced, wearing tiny pink shoes,
Declaring it party time, spreading good news.

And so these secrets twirl round and around,
In the twilight of laughter, joy knows no bounds.
From shadows to silliness, a magical blend,
With each giggle shared, the fun will not end.

Whispers of a Hidden Realm

In a garden of marbles, the flowers wore hats,
Where kittens baked cookies alongside acrobats.
With whispers of pickle, a dance did ignite,
Every fruit in the bowl was at rest for the night.

A turtle named Fred wore a bright polka dot,
He challenged a grasshopper, who jumped to the top.
While the clouds played chess with the ostriches grand,
The gossiping daisies had all made a stand.

With giggles of sunlight and twinkling stars,
The moon had a trampoline, bouncing from Mars.
In a world that was silly, with laughter as glue,
Adventures unraveled with each crazy view.

And as day turned to dusk, their escapades soared,
With secrets unveiled and tales to record.
In whispers of mirth, this realm sings a tune,
Where joy's always shining, from morning till moon.

Dreams Weave Through Gilded Halls

In halls made of biscuits, with laughter as gold,
The carpet was giggling, secrets untold.
With chandeliers waving and curtains that danced,
Even walls rolled their eyes when the cat stole a glance.

A fish in a tuxedo was hosting a game,
While jellyfish juggled without any shame.
With pillows that whispered their fluff and their tales,
The humor was sprinkled like sweet fairy trails.

In the corners, the teacups were spinning in tune,
As muffins recited their sonnets to moon.
And while marshmallows rhymed with bubbly glee,
The laughter echoed, a sweet symphony.

In gilded halls where dreams weave anew,
Joy bottled in whispers, in melodies too.
With a wink and a nod, the night softly falls,
In a dance of delight, where laughter enthralls.

Labyrinth of Lost Lullabies

In a maze where dreams do roam,
Teddy bears have made their home.
Socks play hide and seek with shoes,
While nighttime whispers giggle clues.

The mattress tells a silly tale,
Of pirates feasting on cold kale.
Moonbeams dance on sleeping cats,
As giggles spring from hidden hats.

Jars of jellybeans conspiring,
To take the crown from snoozing king.
In this place of joyful din,
Even snoring sounds like a violin.

Each corner hides a punchline bright,
Where shadows leap and spirits light.
With lullabies that twist and twine,
In a world where silliness is fine.

Fantasies Behind Closed Doors

Behind the door, a jesting cat,
Dances with a hat and bat.
Unicorns bake pies for fun,
While robots bake beneath the sun.

Tickle monsters hold a ball,
As giggles bounce off every wall.
There's a fish who tells a joke,
While rubber chickens serve the yolk.

The couch wears shoes, it's quite a sight,
Playing tag with pillows at night.
Balloons are plotting secret games,
In this world of silly names.

Every latch and every creak,
Whispers secrets, oh so cheek!
Where each adventure's wide and grand,
Dancing dreams across the land.

The Sanctuary of Silent Stories

In a nook where shadows peek,
Books have begun to softly speak.
Penguins in tuxedos pause,
To share their tales with mighty roars.

Underneath the famous shelf,
A dragon dreams of being stealth.
He tickles fairies with his tail,
As whispers ride on paper sail.

Paper boats skip along the floor,
While characters plot their next encore.
The walls erupt with giggling glee,
As stories unfold like summer tea.

Here, every fable has a twist,
And each punchline is hard to miss.
In this haven, fun takes flight,
With magic dancing in the night.

Windows to Unseen Worlds

Through the glass, the sillies peep,
Llamas brush their teeth in sleep.
Giraffes play checkers with the moon,
As clocks sing nutty tunes in tune.

Noses pressed against the frame,
Squirrels plot a wacky game.
Rainbows slide upon the floor,
While giggles stream from every door.

Balloons bounce high with bursts of cheer,
Making friends with frogs who leer.
Funky hats in vibrant hues,
Each window tells a tale of zoos.

With winks from clouds that float about,
And silly shadows that twist and shout.
Every view is pure delight,
In this realm where dreams take flight.

Echoes of Unwritten Stories

In corners where the dust bunnies play,
A tale begins in a most quirky way.
A sock dances with a broken shoe,
While a cat debates what it wants to chew.

The chair whispers secrets to the wall,
As shadows perform a comedic hall.
The fridge hums a tune of forgotten meals,
While laughter bubbles in the air like peels.

If walls could chuckle, would they sigh?
In every crevice, a reason to cry.
For mismatched socks and lost car keys,
Are masterpieces only the cat sees.

So gather your thoughts and look around,
In every silence, a giggle is found.
From wobbly tables to squeaky chairs,
Life's comic script is hidden in layers.

Flickers of Magic in Forgotten Places

In the attic where old memories sleep,
A fairy plays hide and seek with the sheep.
A broom breaksdance with a duster, so fine,
While the clock giggles, losing track of time.

Beneath the bed, a void full of cheer,
With monsters that rhyme, oh so sincere.
They trade their scaring for raucous ballet,
As dust motes twirl in a glittery sway.

The curtains, they whisper tales of delight,
Of laughter and mischief that danced through the night.
The pot plants conspire with the creaky floor,
To brew up a soup called 'fun'—and then more!

In forgotten nooks where enchantment thrives,
Magic ignites as imagination dives.
Where whispers of humor float in the air,
And the ordinary turns wondrously rare.

The Hidden Symphony of the Soul

A spoon sings softly to the sassy fork,
While the kettle tambourines with a cork.
In the rhythm of pots, a story unfolds,
Of ridiculous banquets and comical molds.

The clock ticks tock with a wink and a giggle,
As the toaster pops up, doing a jiggle.
Each wall is a note in a whimsical tune,
With voices that shout, 'Let's dance to the moon!'

Oh, the carpet rolls out its jazz hands with glee,
While the fridge croons sweet melodies, carefree.
In harmony lost, where we stumble and trip,
Laughter becomes our delightful script.

Join the parade of the marvelous shtick,
In kitchens where legends do slapstick!
The unseen laughter holds secrets untold,
Where childhood dreams of nonsense unfold.

Portraits of the Unexplored

In the hallway hangs a puzzle undone,
A mirror reflects a face full of fun.
With hats that are silly and shoes worn askew,
Each glance sparks a giggle from someone like you.

The paintings all wink, inviting a dance,
While a vase struts its stuff, given the chance.
In every shadow, the echoes narrate,
Of pranks played at dusk and odd quirks of fate.

A door creaks open with a laugh and a jive,
Surveying the chaos where whimsy survives.
The closets hold treasures both mixed and absurd,
Like monsters composing a nonsensical word.

So treasure each corner that makes you smile,
For life's a grand canvas; let's paint it in style.
From jester to hero, the stories evolve,
In portraits of moments we gladly resolve.

The Maze of Mysterious Lights

In a place where shadows play,
Lights flicker in a curious way.
Turn left, then right, do a little dance,
You might just find a pair of pants!

A giggle echoes through the haze,
What's that? A cat in a light maze?
It purrs and giggles, it jumps in glee,
It's having more fun than you or me!

Corners hide a rainbow or two,
A little green frog dressed in blue.
He offers you a cupcake treat,
But be careful! It might be your feet!

Laughter bounces from wall to wall,
As you chase lights, you might just fall.
So grab your friends, don't miss the show,
In this maze of laughs, let's go, let's go!

Reflections in a Gilded Mirror

A mirror hangs with a cheeky grin,
Hold still now, let the fun begin!
It shows you things too silly to see,
Like a hat-wearing dog named Freddie!

Your reflection winks and pulls a face,
Twists and turns in a bizarre race.
It says, "Hey you, come dance with me!"
But it's really just your toe that's free!

Clothes become polka-dotted art,
And shoes that wink just fall apart.
"Join me in this wacky style!"
The mirror laughs with a glimmering smile.

Shrieks of laughter spill with cheer,
As colors swirl, they disappear.
But don't fret, just take a chance,
With this mirror, it's a silly dance!

Chronicles of the Unknown

In a book stacked high, tales untold,
Each page flips with a giggle bold.
A dragon wears a bright pink hat,
And writes a letter to a friendly cat!

Places where giants fiddle and sing,
While tiny squirrels plot a prank on spring.
Watch out for gnomes with jellybeans,
They're up to mischief, or so it seems!

A sandwich thief with a peanut butter grin,
Wanders through the chapters, oh what a sin!
He blames the cat for the crumbs all around,
But who really stole the lunch that was found?

Turn the page; get ready to laugh,
For each tale spins a goofy craft.
In the chronicles, chaos reigns,
Grab a seat; let's see the fun it gains!

The Enigma of Painted Skies

Clouds wear hats of purple and gold,
Silly shapes that never get old.
A sunbeam tickles the moonlight's cheek,
While the stars play hide-and-seek!

Raindrops giggle as they fall down,
While puddles turn into a dance floor brown.
Grab your umbrella, let's splash about,
In colors of joy, there's never a doubt!

The wind whispers jokes through the trees,
As birds chirp tunes that aim to please.
And if you listen close, you'll find,
A symphony plays in the back of your mind.

So let's paint the sky with colors bright,
And laugh till the stars are out of sight.
For in this world where whimsy thrives,
The enigma of joy truly arrives!

The Portrait of a Thousand Souls

In a gallery filled with glee,
A painter ran out of tea.
With colors bright, he drew a cat,
And claimed it was his favorite hat.

Each face wore a goofy grin,
As if they'd just won a spin.
One looked like a dancing fool,
Oh, the joy in this crazy school!

A dog in a tux danced all night,
Chasing tails in sheer delight.
The portraits laughed and twirled about,
In a place where joy had no doubt.

And when the moon began to rise,
They threw a party, oh what a surprise!
With silly jokes and cake galore,
A feast to cherish forevermore.

Secrets Beneath the Canopy

Beneath the leaves so lush and green,
A squirrel rehearsed an acrobatic scene.
With a flip and a flop, he jumped with flair,
While nearby owls pretended not to care.

The ants held a meeting, plotting their day,
To carry crumbs in a very odd way.
One slipped and fell, causing quite a fuss,
And the others just laughed, 'Well, that's just us!'

Bees buzzed in laughter, making sweet tunes,
While the raccoon dined under the light of the moons.
They shared silly secrets, under the trees,
In a patchwork of whispers carried by the breeze.

So if you wander where laughter is found,
Join the revelry, let joy abound.
The secrets they keep are silly and bright,
In the canopy's shade, under soft silver light.

The Dance of Ethereal Whispers

In a ballroom of dreams on a starry night,
Whispers twirled in a fanciful flight.
With giggles and chuckles, they floated around,
Two pink unicorns pranced on the ground.

A fairy slipped, her wings in a twist,
'Oops!' she cried, 'How could I miss?'
The gnomes giggled, their potions in hand,
As they wiggled and jiggled, forming a band.

The music was silly, the beat was absurd,
As the trees clapped along, not a soul would deter.
A dance-off began, oh what a sight,
With creatures so strange, both left and right.

So if you hear laughter while dreaming away,
Join the dance, let your worries sway.
In a realm where joy sparkles and glows,
Every wisp is a friend that nobody knows.

The Architect of Mirage

A builder of dreams with a wink and a smile,
Crafted castles from laughter, all the while.
With bricks made of chuckles, they rose to the sky,
He declared, 'What's more fun than watching it fly?'

With a wave of his hand, he drew in the stars,
And painted the moon with giant candy bars.
'Why settle for bland? Let's brighten it up!'
And from thin air, he conjured a cup.

Each room held a theme, a zany delight,
Where jellybeans danced in the pale moonlight.
A slide made of laughter, a floor filled with cheer,
In this architect's world, there's nothing to fear.

So if you stumble upon this strange place,
Where dreams intertwine with a soft, warm embrace,
Just remember the builder, whose heart's all aglow,
In the land of the funny, where wonders flow.

www.ingramcontent.com/pod-product-compliance
Lightning Source LLC
Chambersburg PA
CBHW051734290426
43661CB00123B/272